Law of Attraction Amazing Relationships

How to Drastically Improve Your Love Life and Find Ever-Lasting Happiness with the Law of Attraction!

By Elena G.Rivers

www.LOAforSuccess.com

ISBN-10: 1973987708
ISBN-13: 978-1973987703

Table of Contents

Introduction

Having written numerous books on the Law of Attraction, I have always tried to find a way to explain this topic in a way that was relatable to everyone. When it was suggested that I write about relationships, I knew that I had received my answer.

Any challenge that we have with relationships is due to our lack of understanding of how the Law of Attraction works, that we attracted the people who are in our life, for better or for worse. Unknowingly, most of us try to deal with relationship issues without ever addressing the main source, ourselves.

To deal with relationship issues, we often turn to our friends or experts. Many of us read self-help books, see a counselor, or turn to some spiritual teaching like astrology. Yes, I said "spiritual teaching"! You may be saying to yourself "Wait a minute! Isn't the Law of Attraction a spiritual teaching?" My hope is that, by the time that you finish this book, you will understand what I mean by this statement. While talking to a friend, reading a self-help book, seeing a mental health professional, or turning to a spiritual teaching can be helpful, it is rare that any of these sources can direct us to the root cause of our challenges.

Because we so often restrict our search to the surface level, the frustrations that we experience in our relationships usually live on, despite our best intentions.

It is my hope that the content in this book will trigger the intrinsic knowing that exists within all of us and cause you to remember an essential truth, that you are the creator of all of your experiences. It is only in our amnesia of this truth that we experience frustration or suffering in our lives, which is the purpose of our relationships.

Our relationships are our mirror to our inner selves; they provide us with a glimpse of ourselves that we may otherwise miss.

From the perspective of higher awareness, there is no such thing as a relationship problem. What we call "relationship problems" are really the gifts of the universe that allow us to take a deeper look at ourselves.

Throughout the book, I have used a variety of terms for consciousness, including the greater consciousness, the greater consciousness system, the higher self, or the true self. I have done this just to avoid repetition and to provide variety.

All of these terms refer to the same thing, which is pure consciousness, that which exists beyond our conceptual understanding. If you are ready to take a deep look, I welcome you.

Special Free Offer from Elena to Help You Manifest Faster

Before we jump into it, we would like to offer you a free complimentary workbook. Knowing how to raise your vibration is a very important part of LOA, yet most people struggle with it.

In this short Workbook, I will teach you how to master your energy and vibration, and you can also apply it to your relationships.

You can easily claim it by visiting our private website and joining our free LOA newsletter at:

www.LOAforSuccess.com/newsletter

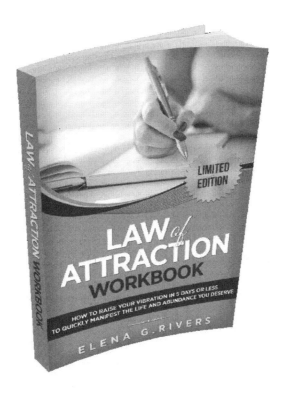

You will also be the first one to learn about my new releases, giveaways, bonuses and other valuable resources to help you on your journey.

Sign up now and I'll "see you" in the first email.

Love,

Elena

Chapter 1: Thoughts, Beliefs, and Reality

We will start off this chapter with an exercise. Sit down, make yourself comfortable, and close your eyes.

1. I want you to imagine a full moon. Make this image as real as possible.
   Note: Everyone visualizes differently. The visualizations of some people are vivid, while those of others may be blurry or murky. Just visualize the way that is natural for your and trust yourself.
2. Now, I want you to visualize a red sports car, making it as real as possible.
3. Finally, I want you to visualize a red rose.
4. Now open your eyes.

Did you learn anything from this exercise? If you are unable to answer this question, do not let it bother. Most people would have difficulty answering it. So, just in case, let me help you by guiding you to the answer.

First of all, you imagined a full moon, a red sports car, and a red rose. Most likely, you did not confuse any of these images with who you are. You did not think that you were the full moon, the red sports car, or the red rose. Why didn't you? There are two reasons for this. The first reason was that you were the observer of these images. Second, these images lacked significant meaning for you. You are not your thoughts! You are the observer of thoughts.

The challenge that we face is that we often forget that we are not our thoughts. It was easy for you to understand this when doing this exercise, but what about the times when you are experiencing thoughts of anger, frustration, concern, jealousy, or fear?

During these times, it is very easy to get caught-up in our thoughts. If we have thoughts of anger, we become anger. If we have thoughts of insecurity, we become insecurity, and so on. All these thoughts are no different than the thoughts of the full moon, the red sports car, or the red rose. Regardless of the thought that you have, you are not it.

The ancient Greek philosopher Plato put forth a theory which he termed the "Allegory of the Cave." This allegory was intended to cause the listener of his teaching to question the accuracy of their perceptions and thinking and look toward a more reliable truth. In his analogy, he proposed a scenario where he asked his student to imagine a cave which is inhabited by people. These people were born in the cave and had never experienced the world outside of it. In fact, they are not even aware of its existence. The people in the cave are chained in a manner that the only direction they can look toward is the back of the cave. They are unable to view the mouth of the cave.

Unbeknownst to the people in the cave, there is a fire that continually burns near the mouth of the cave. Anytime a person or animal passes between the fire and the mouth of the cave; their shadows are cast against the back of the cave. The people of the cave believe that the projected shadows are real, that they are actual beings that also inhabit the cave.

One day, one of the cave people managed to break out of his chains and ventured out of the cave. He was bewildered by the new world that he saw, believing that it was some illusion.

As he became more familiar with this new world, he began to realize that this new world was not an illusion, that it was the shadows on the cave's wall that were illusionary.

This denizen of the cave who broke out of his chains and ventured into the outside had expanded his level of awareness. It took a totally different experience for him to gain the understanding that he had believed in the illusions of the shadows for all of his life.

The chains that bounded this person are also part of the metaphor in that they represent our experience of life when we trust our misperceptions. It is only when we have the courage to venture out of the cave that we experience a greater truth, which requires us to break the chains that are holding us. What are these chains that are binding us? Essentially, it is our fear and our conditioning.

The analogy of the cave is a great metaphor for understanding how we are affected by our thoughts and perceptions. An understanding of the illusionary quality our thoughts and perceptions are essential if we are to understand the Law of Attraction and how it impacts our relationships. But before we go any further, let us consider another analogy for challenging our notions of reality, which everyone can relate to.

Most of us believe that our everyday experience of life is ultimate reality, that how we experience ourselves and the world around us is reality. Consider this: When you have a dream, doesn't it become your reality while you are experiencing it? What about when you have a nightmare? Can anyone who has ever had a nightmare deny that the experience was real for them? Some nightmares are so vivid that even when we wake-up we experience moments of disorientation and confusion.

When we have a dream, we are projecting our thoughts, which we experience as our dream self and its dream world. I used to have reoccurring dreams where I could fly to get from place to place. With each place I flew to, I engaged with other dream characters and dream environments.

In one dream, I descended onto a busy market place in some third world country. I experienced a vibrant and bustling market place where other dream characters were going about their business. Further, my experience of myself was very real. I had thoughts, experienced feelings, and emotions, and I took action in this dream world.

All of these experiences were a projection of my consciousness. When I woke up the next morning, I realized it was just a dream and experienced the reality of my waking world. But who can say that our waking world is not just another dream?

Who can say that our experience of daily life is just another projection of some greater truth? Some of you may make the argument that our waking life is real because we live it every day; we are working, taking care of our families, and making important decisions. But don't these things occur in our dreams as well?

I present to you these scenarios for one reason, which is this: How we experience our relationships, and anything else in life, is based on how we interpret the information that is contained in your experience. How you interpret the information of your experiences is based on our beliefs, the same beliefs that led the cave denizens to believe that the shadows were actual beings or for me to believe that I was flying in a third world marketplace. My question to you is what beliefs do you hold to that are hindering or empowering your relationships?

When you have an issue in your relationship, what thoughts or beliefs do you normally experience? Do you frequently experience thoughts like:

- "I cannot believe he did that!"
- *"She is always nagging or criticizing me."*
- "Does he love me?"
- *"Why did he say that?"*
- "She does not believe me."
- *"I can't trust him."*
- "He never tells me what is going on."
- *"I wish he would be closer to me."*
- "Men, they are all alike."
- *"Women, they are all like."*
- "I do not think he loves me."

Regardless of the thought, you have about your relationship, if you regularly give it your attention, you strengthen that thought. There is a metaphor that I once heard that I really like regarding a table. Imagine that thought is like the legs of a table. If you have a particular thought about your relationship, which occasionally arises in your awareness, it is like a table top with only a single leg attached to it.

A table top with a single leg is not stable and can easily collapse. Now imagine that you experience something in your relationship that reinforces that thought, now is as though you have two table legs supporting the table top.

For example, you occasionally wonder if your boyfriend or girlfriend is taking you for granted; however, you do not take that thought seriously. Then one day, he or she seems to blow you off when you are obviously having a bad day. Your original thought has a new reference point that strengthens or confirms your original thought.

Now let us say several other incidents occur where you feel like you are being taken for granted. These additional incidents are like the third and fourth table leg. Now the table top stands steady; it is firmly established. The table top in this metaphor is what we refer to as a belief. A belief is a thought which you have a sense of certainty about as being true.

Now let us shift from metaphor to how your thoughts actually work. To begin with, your thoughts are nothing but bits of information, which you attract to you. What causes thoughts to be attracted to you is the attention that you give them. I use the words "are attracted to you" for a specific reason. Though it may be difficult to believe, particularly in the early stages of this book, you do not have thoughts! Your brain does not create thoughts!

You can think of thoughts as a signal from a cell phone tower. In this metaphor, you are the cell phone. Just as signals from the cell phone towers are received by the cell phone, the bits of information that you receive, known as thoughts, is received by you.

You may be wondering where the thoughts that you receive come from. The answer to that question will be discussed later on in this book. For now, know that you do not create your thoughts; you are the one that attracts them through your attention.

Your thoughts are powerless in that they lack any inherent power of their own. The only power that our thoughts have is the power that we give them through our attention.

So let us return to the previous example that you believe that the person you are having a relationship with is taking you for granted.

That belief started off with a thought, which you were entertaining. Because you gave this thought your attention, it energized it, giving it some power. Because it became energized, that thought attracted other thoughts that were of similar quality. Your original thought "I think my partner is taking me for granted" attracted other thought of the same energetic level, such as "He or she did not bother to inquire how I was feeling."

Because you gave that thought your attention, it attracted the next thought, perhaps "He did not ask if he could do anything to make me feel better." In this manner, our thoughts are like a magnet that attracts iron filings. Just as iron filings accumulate around the magnet, the original thought that you continually gave your attention to attract an army of other thoughts of like quality.

Now let us use another scenario, using the same theme as the last one. In this scenario, you are feeling down and there is someone, who you have absolutely no interest in, who totally ignores you. The fact that this person is ignoring you does not disturb you a bit. In fact, you are glad he or she is not trying to interact with you because you have no desire to talk to this person. Your attention is no longer attracting the thought " He is taking me for granted." Because you do not give this thought your attention, it fails to carry any potency in our conscious awareness. Why is this information important to understand? Well, there are a number of reasons, which we will discuss later in this book. For now, let us focus on the power that beliefs have on our lives.

You can think of beliefs as colored tinted sunglasses. If you wear sunglasses that are tinted yellow, then everything that you experience will appear to be yellow in color. If you wear red tinted sunglasses, everything will appear to be red. Just as tinted sunglasses color the world that we see, our beliefs color our experience of life, especially our relationships.

Whatever belief you have about your relationship, it will color every aspect of your relationship. Your beliefs determine what you focus on in your relationship; they will determine how you feel about your relationship; they will determine the decisions that you make about your relationship, and they will determine the kind of actions that you will take regarding your relationship.

The question is what happens if your beliefs are not accurate? Once you believe something with conviction, it is extremely difficult to see any other perspective, even when your perspective does not accurately reflect how the other person feels.

When you proclaim that you know what another person is thinking or feeling, and they tell you otherwise, you will conclude that they are not honest with you, when in fact they may be very sincere.

Does this mean that you should never trust your beliefs and believe whatever they say? No, of course not! We will explore this further later on. For now, realize that each one of us creates our own unique perspective on our experience in life.

The perspective that each one of us has is determined by the beliefs that we hold, and the beliefs that we hold are based on the thoughts that we attract, which brings us to the Law of

Attraction. The thoughts that you attract is just one example of the Law of Attraction in action.

Each person is giving their attention to a particular thought, which is attracting other thoughts. It is through the attraction of thoughts that each one of us creates our own unique perspective.

 Is because of this simple fact that relationships always have and will always be complicated; they are complicated because no two persons in the history of this planet will ever share the exact same perspective. What may seem to be a cruel joke on the part of the universe is actually a gift.

We will discuss this soon in another chapter. For now, we need to talk about emotions, which is the subject of the next chapter.

Chapter 2: The Link between Thoughts and Emotions

In the previous chapter, it was explained that our thoughts are bits of information that we attract through our attention. Our emotions are a mirror to our thought, or we could say that our emotions are a message to us indicating the kinds of thoughts that we are experiencing.

We may not always know the thoughts that we are experiencing, especially if they are subconscious; however, our emotions will inform us to the kind of thoughts that we are experiencing, regardless if we are aware of our thoughts or not. If you are experiencing the emotion of anger, it is because you are having thoughts of anger.

It is important that we further explore the statement that I made regarding "thoughts of anger." Let me begin by saying that there are no angry thoughts, nor are there happy thoughts or thoughts that depict any other kind of emotion.

Thoughts are just bits of information that we process, just as information is processed by a computer. The information in your computer is not bad or good, happy or sad, frustrated or relaxed; it is just information. Similarly, your thoughts are just information. We create "happy thoughts" or "sad" thoughts by projecting meaning on to our thoughts. To better understand this, let us look back in history to a famous experiment.

Ivan Pavlov was a Russian scientist who conducted an experiment to demonstrate conditioning. Pavlov would show a piece of meat to a dog, which caused the dog to salivate. The dog had become conditioned to associate meat with food as part of its evolution in becoming a predator. Pavlov would then ring a bell at the same time that he presented meat to the dog. He would do this repeatedly, present the meat while ringing the bell. With time, Pavlov only had to ring the bell and the dog would salivate.

Originally, the bell would not elicit any response from the dog. It was after repeatedly pairing the bell with the meat that the bell took on a new meaning for the dog. In the same way, your thoughts are like the bell before it was linked to the meat. After repeated experience, you had learned to associate meaning to your thoughts.

Simply stated, nothing in this world has inherent meaning to it. Rather, it is you that creates the meaning of your thoughts; thus, your experience. Since your emotions are a mirror of your thoughts, you also create the meaning that you experience through your emotions.

Returning to our original scenario of "my partner takes me for granted," the person who had this thought was projecting it on her partner. She created the meaning and then projected it on him; just as when I projected my thoughts and created an alternate reality where I was flying to a third world market place while dreaming.

Chapter 3: Who Are You?

The question of who you are is the most important question that you will ever ask. No question can ever be more meaningful than this one. I do not care if someone is a great scientist, a great philosopher, or a world leader. Without understanding who we are, we are no better than the people of the Allegory of the Cave. Just as the shadows were the reality of the people in the cave, we take our experiences to be reality. Before we can understand our perceived reality, we need to understand the perceiver.

Unless we do this, we are like the shadow gazers in the cave or the one who wears yellow tinted sunglasses and believes the world is yellow. The quality of your relationships will reach new heights when you first learn to understand yourself.

Who is the one that is aware of this book that you are reading? Who is the one who could conjure up images of a full moon, a red sports car, or a red rose? Who is the one that was aware that you were neither of these things? Who is the one that is aware of thought, perception, or sensation?

Who are the one that is aware of the dream world and the awakening from it? The most obvious answer to these questions would be "I am," or "Me." Yet, you are aware of this as well. Who is aware of "I am" or "Me"? The words "I am" or

"Me" are just thoughts or concepts; yet, there is awareness of them.

I have had out of body experiences before. I was aware of being out of body, and I knew when I returned to my body. Who was the one that was aware of these things? When you go into deep sleep, beyond any dream, you have entered a realm that is devoid of all thought.

Because there is no thought, there is no sense of experience. Since there is no experience, there is no memory of deep sleep. Yet, you know that you had experienced it. Who is the one that is aware of deep sleep? If you continue to respond to these questions with answers like "I am," "Me," "my mind," or "I don't know," who is the one that is aware of these answers?

The answer to all of these questions cannot be found by thinking about it. Any answer that you could give is recognized or known by you. Who are you? How can you be anything that you are aware of?

There is the one that is aware and there is the object of awareness. Any answer that you can give is an object in your awareness; otherwise, you would not be aware of it! Rather than just reading about it, I want you to start experiencing for yourself what I am talking about.

1. Sit down, make yourself comfortable, and close your eyes.

2. Breathing normally, place your attention on your breath. Your only job is to be aware of the sensations that you experience as your breath travels in and out of your body during inhalation and exhalation.

3. At some point, you will get distracted by your thoughts. Do not try to control or stop your thoughts. It will not work! Rather than trying to do battle with your thoughts, offer them your complete acceptance.

4. As soon as you acknowledge your thoughts, return your attention back to your breath. No matter how many times you get distracted by your thought, just return your attention back to your breath.

5. Do not judge anything that you experience. Do not try to control or resist any of your experiences. Do not try to use your imagination or try to make things happen. Just observe your experiences through your awareness of it. To be aware of anything is to know of its existence.

6. The more you catch yourself getting distracted by your thoughts, the better you will become in recognizing that you have become distracted without getting caught up in them. The more you practice this exercise, the calmer your mind will become.

When you start experiencing a calmer mind, take your experience as step further by doing the next exercise.

Part 2

1. Sit down, make yourself comfortable, and close your eyes.

2. Breathing normally, place your attention on your breath. Your only job is to be aware of the sensations that you experience as your breath travels in and out of your body during inhalation and exhalation.

3. If you get distracted by your thoughts, just return your attention back to your breath. As your mind becomes calmer, remove your focus from your breath and allow yourself just to relax. Do not try to focus on anything. Just remain aware of anything that you experience.

4. Be aware of any sensations that you experience.

5. Be aware of the coming and going of thought.

6. Be aware of any perceptions or images that may appear.

7. Be aware of the sounds that you hear in your surroundings.

8. Be aware of all that you experience.

9. Do not try to identify, analyze, or get curious about anything that you experience. Do not engage in any thinking. Just observe.

10. There can be no experience without the awareness of it. Can you find that which is aware of all that you experience?

Chapter 4: The Law of Attraction Works through You!

In the last exercise, were you able to identify that which is aware of all of your experiences? If you were not able to, know that you are on the right track.

That which is aware of all of your experiences is your most essential nature. Who you are is beyond any thought that you could ever conceive. Who you are is beyond anything that you could ever experience. Who you are is awareness itself!

The advance of the sciences, such as quantum physics, has demonstrated that the world of form is just an illusion. The world of form is like the shadows in the allegory of the cave.

It has been discovered that the atom, once formerly believed to be a solid structure, is now known to be formless. In other words, the building blocks of all physical form are nonphysical! You are no different. Though you may believe that you are physical being, this belief is only a half truth. You are a multi-dimensional being in that you are both physical and a non-physical at the same time.

In your physical dimension, you experience yourself as being a unique and separate individual who lives amid a physical world with other physical beings. In your nonphysical dimension, you do not exist as an individual being as your most essential is that of oneness. Popular expressions such as "God is love" or "Everything is One" refers to your nonphysical dimension. Everything that exists in the physical realm merges into the non-physical. Conversely, the non-physical realm is the source of the physical realm. At the non-physical level, there is no individualization or separation, at this level, there is no sense of relationship.

For a relationship to exist, there must be a sense of separation. You experience yourself having a relationship with other people because you experience yourself as being separate from them.

How can there be a relationship when there is no sense of separation? Without a sense of separation, there is no "you and me" or "us and them," there is only energy and information. The basis of the entire universe is energy and information; everything that appears to be physical is simply a temporary manifestation of this energy and information. That which we refer to as love, especially the higher forms of love (as opposed to conditional love), is referring to this energy and information. It is referred to as love because it is totally inclusive, all encompassing, and whole.

If you were able to successfully do the last meditation, you were fully aware of all of your thoughts, sensations, and perceptions. Not only were you fully aware of them, but you also offered complete acceptance of their existence. These are the qualities of inclusiveness and all encompassing. Your experience was inclusive because you did not judge any of your experiences. Your experience was all encompassing because you were aware of all of your experiences. If you experienced a sense of wholeness, it was because you were not experiencing any scarcity, needing, or desire. Your experience was enough for you to feel complete.

The non-physical aspect of you is consciousness, and it is the purpose of consciousness is to expand. Expansion can only come about through the encountering of experience.

Since the nature of your highest aspect is oneness, consciousness differentiates itself by manifesting into physical form. By taking on a physical form, a sense of separateness appears, and a sense of separateness creates experience. It is through the act of experiencing that information is gained. The gaining of information is what leads to the expansion of consciousness.

Every experience that you have leads to the gaining of new information and that new information leads to the expansion of consciousness, not only in your physical form, but in the larger consciousness system.

The quality of information that you provide the consciousness system determines if whether you are evolving into love (the larger consciousness system) or if you are becoming further removed from it and staying identified with your physical form, which leads to suffering. We suffer because we identify with our physical form, which is the result of the ego. Since we identify with our minds and bodies, we experience a lack of wholeness, that something is missing from our lives. We seek out relationships in our attempts to regain that sense of wholeness.

Because most of us have identified with our minds and bodies, we have forgotten our connection to the larger consciousness system, which is our essential self. With that forgetfulness, we have lost our sense of connection with the rest of the universe.

There is nothing special about the Law of Attraction, and it is operating in our lives at every moment. The basis of the universe is energy and that energy contains the potential to manifest itself in infinite ways.

Your manifested form, your physical body, is made of energy, the same energy that belongs to the larger consciousness system. You are no more separate from the larger consciousness than a drop of ocean water is from the ocean itself.

However, as a manifested form, you have qualities about you that the larger consciousness does not have.

The larger consciousness is pure, without any form distinction or differentiation; it is oneness. In your manifested form, that pure consciousness becomes conditioned by the thoughts and beliefs that we adopt.

Just as Pavlov's dog became conditioned to salivate at the sound of a bell, we have become conditioned to believe that we are our minds and bodies.

The conditioned consciousness takes on different qualities and those different qualities of consciousness attract other forms of energy that are of a like kind. Let's examine this more closely using examples that we can easily identify with:

Alice grew up in an environment, where she was deprived of attention and warmth. Alice's essential being is that of pure consciousness. Alice's physical being is a localized expression of her higher self. Additionally, Alice, like most of us, identifies with her physical form; she believes that she is her thoughts and physical body.

Because she did not receive attention and warmth as a child, she developed beliefs about herself like: "Expressing warmth and vulnerability is scary" and " I am not lovable." These beliefs condition her consciousness in a way that her life's energy will attract those things into her life whose' energy is of like quality. When it comes to relationships, she will attract those partners who also resist expressing warmth and vulnerability, which will reinforce her beliefs that she is unlovable. Should a partner express warmth and vulnerability, it will create discomfort within her because she does not know how to act.

Energy cannot be created or destroyed; the only thing that it can do is to take on a different form. Let us imagine that year's pass and the energy that Alice repressed (by fearing warmth or vulnerability) finally takes its toll. Alice experiences some major life changes, and she is unable to handle those changes emotionally.

She has hit bottom; her pain is so great that she gets professional help. She gradually learns to stop repressing her feelings and gains the courage to express them. All those years of resisting the experiencing of her emotions and feelings have reached their breaking point.

By allowing herself to express and experience them, her life's energy takes on new quality, one that will attract into her life those relationships and conditions that are consistent with her higher level of energy.

In Chapter 1, we discussed the nature of thoughts, emotions; however, we did not discuss feelings. Now it's the perfect time to do so. Your feelings are your direct connection to the greater consciousness. When you are experiencing feelings of frustration, fear, anxiety, or concern, you are out of alignment with your higher self. When you are experiencing feelings of well-being, joy, love, or appreciation, you are aligned with your higher self or greater consciousness.

One of the most valuable things that you can do to effectively attract that which you desire, including the relationships that you want, is to develop greater awareness of your thoughts, emotions, and feelings for they are an indicator of what you are attracting into your life.

As stated earlier, you are always attracting things into your life, whether you believe in the Law of Attraction or not. It is like gravity. Whether you believe in gravity or not, gravity affects you. The only difference between someone who consciously applies the Law of Attraction and someone who does not is the quality of their experience.

The first person will attract into their life a broad range of beneficial experiences that support them in their growth as an evolved human, while those who are not conscious of the Law of Attraction will judge themselves or their experience as a reflection of their self-worth, as well as being out of their control.

While the first person understands that they are responsible for what they attract, the latter will blame their misfortune on others, bad luck, or themselves. When we blame ourselves, we believe that we are not worthy, which lowers our vibration.

In writing that the first person understands that they are responsible for what they attract, I do not mean this in a way that implies morality or guilt. Rather, they take responsibility in that they are aware of the vibrational level of their life and change it as needed so that they are attracting that which they intend.

Chapter 5: The Vibrational Level of Your Life

I will be using terms like vibrational level or frequency often in this book, so now is the time to clarify what I mean by these terms.

There is nothing abstract or mysterious about these terms; we experience them on a moment by moment basis. As mentioned earlier, everything in existence is comprised of energy, so your vibrational level or frequency is the quality of your energy.

You experience this energy through your thoughts, emotions, and feelings. To be aware of your vibrational level or frequency is to be aware of your thoughts, emotions, and feelings. The quality of these three phenomena reflects the quality of your experience of life, including your relationships. This becomes very obvious when you look at the quality of your relationships or in the relationships of those who you know. The following are just a few hypothetical examples of how the quality of life's energy attracts those of like kind:

- A woman, who feels insecure and significant, enters a relationship with a man who becomes abusive toward her. Her low vibrational energy makes her an easy target for him, while his low vibrational energy causes him to control her so that he can feel a sense of power.

- *A woman, who wants to feel complete, feels that being married to a rich and successful husband will make her happy. She meets such a man and gets married to him. What she does not realize is that he also wants to feel complete. In order to feel complete, he is super focused on achieving, in order to feel better about himself. Since he has little time for her, she remains feeling incomplete.*

- A very attractive woman has a best friend who is very plain looking. The attractive woman is tired of the attention she gets from men, making her feel uncomfortable. Further, she finds that other women become jealous of her because of her look. Her plain friend wants to remain inconspicuous because he does not fecl desirable.

A man, who has had limited experience with women in the past, desperately wants a girlfriend.

He meets a woman who has recently broken up with her boyfriend. She wants to be in a relationship because she does not like being alone and seeks her security by being in a relationship.

Both of these people enter the relationship with an energy that is low in vibration as it is based on fear and need. At first, they cannot get enough of each other and the relationship seems perfect, that is until their needs for being in a relationship is met. When this need is met, they realize how neither one of them are getting their needs met. Their needs for being in a relationship was met, but their relationship needs were not.

The point is simple; there are no accidents in this life. Every person that enters your life is there for a reason. In the next chapter, we will explore why every person that enters your life is a gift to you from the universe.

There is a term that is commonly used in the spiritual community, which I want to challenge, that term is the "twin flame." This term refers to the belief that there is one person in this life that is your perfect match. It is my argument that the whole idea of a "twin flame" is just a romantic notion. From the perspective of the Law of Attraction, every person that you meet is your perfect match, though that may seem otherwise.

Remember, at the level of the greater consciousness there is only oneness; It is in our physical manifestation that we experience separation, which creates a sense of relationship between you and others. It is in your relationships, be they casual or intimate, that lead to the expansion of consciousness, both at the individual and cosmic level.

 It is only through you interacting with others that the expansion of the universe can occur.

Your perfect mirror

Earlier, I offered you a metaphor of your relationship to the greater consciousness, which was a drop of seawater in the ocean. While it may seem insignificant, a drop of sea water has the same composition as the ocean itself.

When the greater consciousness differentiated itself, leading to your physical manifestation, you became a localized aspect of the greater consciousness. As the drop is to the ocean, you are to the greater consciousness.

The greater consciousness differentiated itself so that it could experience contrast through experience. You have probably heard adages such as "You cannot know the light unless you first know the dark," or "You cannot know peace unless you first experience war."

 These adages are referring to contrast. It is only through contrast that the higher self can experience itself, which leads to its expansion. The greater consciousness system is unable to experience contrast because it's nature is oneness, which is why it appears in manifested forms, as with you and I.

Experience occurs when there is contrast, and experience leads to the creation of information. Imagine a small child who has never seen a stove. The child touches the stove and burns itself. The child has just experienced contrast: The absence of pain and the existence of pain. This contrast creates experience. Further, the child gains information, which is that stoves are hot. You are the interface that makes it possible for your higher self to learn about its own existence!

When the larger consciousness gains its formation from your experience, it creates experiences that are consistent with the information that it has received.

What is the information that consciousness receives that determines the experiences that it creates for you? The answer to that question is your vibrational energy, which you experience as your thoughts, emotions, and feelings.

We have already discussed the basics of thoughts, emotions, and feelings. In the next chapter, we will discuss their vibrational quality and how they affect your ability to attract that which you want in your life.

Chapter 6: About your Vibe

In this chapter, we will discuss how thoughts and emotions contribute to your vibrational level.

Thoughts

It is a popular misconception that we attract into our life that which we think of, that our thoughts are what creates our manifestations. While our thoughts are definitely a component of the manifestation process, what is even more powerful is our emotions and feelings. If you are looking to find inner peace, a sense of well-being, or to become a conscious manifester, the less that you depend on your thoughts, the better you will be.

Depending on our thoughts to manifest is unreliable because our thoughts are unreliable. Our minds are all about self-preservation, the preservation of our ego. Let me share with you an example of this from my own experience when I was just starting off learning about the Law of Attraction.

I meditated to develop a quiet mind and then made the intention that I wanted to know what book or magazine cover I would encounter when I went to the library that day. I received an image of the cover that I would see, after which I quickly forgot about it. When I got to the library, I walked around the book aisles just to browse (I had forgotten about my intention). As I browsed, I came across a magazine that the same cover that I had experienced in my meditation. It was a cover that I had never seen before, other than in my meditation.

I was so excited that I had successfully manifested intentionally! I then decided to test my abilities out again. I went into my meditation and made an intention that I wanted to see a certain object when I was out and about. At first, I did not think about the object but then my mind got actively involved. I was actively looking for the object, which later led me to start doubting myself. Needless to say, I never encountered the object.

There is a term in spirituality known as detachment, the ability to not cling on to anything, including our thoughts. Detachment was a characteristic of my first manifesting experience; it definitely was not in my second experience.

The challenge to developing detachment is that it takes practice and patience as it is very easy to engage with the mind when you are trying to practice detachment.

The second challenge of relying on thoughts for manifesting is that there may be thoughts that we are not aware of. Subconscious thoughts, more accurately known as subconscious beliefs, can easily act as a counter force against any conscious thoughts that you may have.

Emotions

Your emotions are a more dependable and a more effective point of focus than your thoughts alone. First of all, your emotions are a reflection of your beliefs. The second advantage is that by focusing on your emotions, you remove your focus from your thoughts. The advantage of this is that you remove yourself from the influence of the ego. The following is a list of emotions that are ranked according to their vibrational level.

1. Apathy
2. Shame
3. Guilt
4. Grief
5. Fear
6. Anger
7. Acceptance
8. Joy
9. Gratitude
10. Appreciation
11. Love/Compassion
12. Enlightenment

Apathy: Apathy is ranked the lowest of the emotions on the list because all emotional connection is cut off when we are experiencing apathy. Apathy is a condition where emotions are suppressed. Since emotions are energy, apathy is the suppression of energy.

Shame: The emotion of shame is the second lowest emotion as it involves negatively focusing on yourself. Since you are energizing the low-frequency thoughts that you have of yourself, you are attracting other thoughts of the same frequency.

Earlier in this book, I had you imagine a full moon a red sports car, and a red rose. You were to focus on these images; yet, you did not identify with these images, at no time did you believe that you were these images. These images were a form of thought. Unlike these thoughts, you experience other thoughts which you do identify with. If you ever found yourself caught up in anger, jealousy, or frustration, you had identified with a thought. The emotion of shame takes self-identification to an all time low.

Guilt: Guilt is the next lowest emotion because guilt, like shame, a degree of identification with the ego. The emotion of guilt is intended to be a message to you that you need to change your beliefs about your relationship toward other people. If you change your beliefs for more empowering ones, then guilt has performed its function. If you dwell on how inadequate you are as a human being, you have thrown yourself to the mercy of your mind. Where shame is based on self-worth, guilt is more based on behavior.

Grief: Grief is the emotion of loss and the sense of loss is based on a sense of separation. From the point of higher levels of consciousness, it is impossible to experience grief because the sense of separation does not exist.

Fear: While grief is the emotion of loss, fear is the anticipation of loss. One of the biggest challenges in a relationship is based on fear, the fear of losing an aspect of ourselves and the fear of losing the other person.

Anger: Anger is a reaction to fear, and it has a higher frequency than fear. We experience anger because we feel something that we have identified with is being threatened. If you did not feel identified with that which is being threatened, you would not be angry. You would most likely not feel angry if someone rear ended another driver; you are more likely to experience anger if the car that was rear ended is yours.

Satisfaction: The emotion of satisfaction is a higher vibration than anger because it involves less identification. Both anger and fear are experienced as result of identifying with something outside ourselves. The emotion of satisfaction is an indicator that the emotion of fear is temporarily absent. While a higher frequency than anger, the emotion of satisfaction will be fleeting as long as we continued to identify with our thoughts or the people and objects around us.

Happiness: The frequency of the emotion of happiness is higher than satisfaction; however, the happiness that most of us experience is dependent on the conditions of our life being to our liking, which is a challenge given that everything in the phenomenal world undergoes change. To seek out relationships for the purpose of finding happiness is like building sand castles on the ocean edge; it will remain standing only till the next wave.

Joy: Joy is a higher vibration than happiness; however, it is an unstable emotion if the source of joy is found outside of us.

Gratitude: Gratitude is a higher vibratory level than joy because gratitude is an energy that focuses on the people, animals, or objects around us. Because it has an outward focus, it is a more stable energy frequency. The problem with gratitude is that it is often expressed in response to the receiving of a gift. For this reason, it is an energy frequency that is still vulnerable to changes in external conditions.

Appreciation: Appreciation is a higher frequency than gratitude because the emotion of appreciation can be experienced independently of any external conditions. For example, we can have an appreciation for a beautiful sunset or the work of an artist.

Love: We frequently think of love as being the most powerful force in the universe, which is true, if that love is unconditional. Since the love that we experience is normally conditional, it is subject to the changes of our external conditions, such as when our partner does not meet our expectations.

Enlightenment: Enlightenment has the highest vibratory level of any energy. Unconditional love can be equated with enlightenment; however, enlightenment can be achieved without first developing unconditional love, which is extremely rare. A more practical approach to enlightenment can be achieved by practicing meditation and self-inquiry. Both of these practices can lead to the expansion of awareness where we come to the realization that who we are is beyond our mind and body. However, this awareness must be achieved through the direct experience of it; it cannot be achieved intellectually or by reading about it. In the exercise portion of this book, I have offered exercises for this.

In my discussion of the energy levels of the various emotions, you may have noticed a pattern. The lower the emotion, the lower the vibrational level or frequency. The reason why the frequency is low is due to the amount of identification with the mind and body, which leads to a sense of separateness.

Because we experience separateness, we are reactive when the conditions around us change.

The higher the vibrational level of the emotion, the less identification there is to the mind and body; hence, we become less reactive toward changes in our circumstances.

Someone who is fearful or has not allowed themselves to grieve (as in the death of a partner) have a low life frequency as they deeply identify with their thoughts and emotions. A common example of this is the person who feels that they need to be in a relationship in order to feel good about themselves.

If they find a relationship with another person, that person will have the same energy level as they do, though they may express their neediness differently. They may have a need to control or take advantage of other person in their attempts to feel more powerful.

Now consider the person who focuses on understanding themselves, instead of finding a relationship. If they practice meditation, their life's energy will be at higher levels; hence, they will attract someone whose life's energy is also high. It is impossible for a person of a high frequency to attract a person of low frequency, or a low frequency person to attract a high-level one.

Attracting a healthy and fulfilling relationship requires that we focus on raising our life first, while the norm for society is to seek out a relationship in order to feel better about ourselves.

The Mirror of Relationships

The greater consciousness, whose' quality is oneness, differentiates itself into localized consciousness in order to gain information through the experience of contrast. We can think of the greater consciousness as a CEO of a major company.

For him or her to understand what is happening in the company, he relies on numerous individuals that serve beneath him. Each of these individuals has a specific task that they are responsible for. In order to accomplish their tasks, they need to interact act with others, which creates the experience of contrast.

How can the CEO understand anything about the sales of the company if he or she does not have a sales report? For this information to be generated, there needs to be individuals who are conducting sales. For sales to be created, there needs to be interactions between the sales people and their clients. The conducting of sales with clients is an experience of contrast as the client needs to determine if agreeing to buy will create added value for him or her. The decisions that are made at this level inform the CEO of the sales of the company.

Another metaphor for the larger consciousness system is from physicist Tom Campell who compares the larger consciousness system to a video game. You in your manifested form are like the avatar in the video game, while the larger consciousness system is the one who is playing the video game.

The virtual environment provides a context for the avatar to interact in, while the joy stick symbolizes the intentions of the larger consciousness.

When the avatar interacts with its environment in ways that earn points, that information provides feedback to the video game player. If the avatar interacts with its environment in a manner that leads to its destruction, then that information is provided to the player. Similarly, every moment that you are interacting with your environment informs the greater consciousness. The larger consciousness continuously responds back to this feedback by creating experiences that are consistent with the feedback that it has received.

We are localized aspects of consciousness that interact with each other for the purpose of creating experiences of contrast, which in turn informs the larger consciousness system to the nature of itself. Each person that we interact with is an experience in contrast that informs the larger consciousness system. Here is an example:

Jon and his wife are having an argument over an incident; he took offense over something that she said to him.

Jon perceives his wife as the source of his upset. His upset is a natural reaction given that Jon identifies himself with his mind and body, meaning that Jon believes that he is the culmination of his thoughts, emotions, perceptions, and his sense of physicality.

This self-identification creates a sense of separation where he experiences his wife as being a separate individual that exists apart from him. Since she is the one that made the comment, and he is the one that felt offended, he believes that she is the cause of his upset.

From the perspective of higher levels of consciousness, a whole different story is unfolding. Jon's wife is serving as a mirror to Jon's vibratory level.

Just as the bell was a stimulus that activated a response in Pavlov's dog, his wife's comments acted as a stimulus to activate Jon's life condition.

The comments made by Jon's wife were not the initial cause for Jon feeling offended. Rather, the initial cause for Jon's offense took place far earlier in his life, perhaps in a different lifetime even. Regardless of when that initial cause occurred, it was the result of Jon self-identifying with his mind and body.

However, this self-identification is not a mistake of the universe, nor is it a mistake on our part; rather, it is part of the process of the evolution of consciousness.

Chapter 7: Love: The Evolution of Consciousness

Remember the previous example of the CEO? How does the CEO know if the sales strategy of his company is working or not? He or she knows this by whether or not they are getting the results that they want. There is a term in science called entropy.

While there are several definitions for entropy, one definition involves the simplicity or complexity of a system. The qualities of greater consciousness are of oneness and inclusiveness, making it a low entropy system.

As entrophy increases, the system increasingly experiences disorder. High entropy systems consume a lot of energy while low entropy systems are energy efficient. Systems are constantly fluctuating between high and low entropy.

The relationships in our lives, along with other forms of experience, are a mirror for us to examine our own energy level based on how we respond to ourselves and others. In a previous section, we discussed the frequencies of different emotions. Shame has a very low frequency while appreciation is very high. Which emotion do you think consumes a great deal of energy and which one do you think is energy efficient? To answer that question, all you have to do is ask yourself how you feel during these times. Which of these emotions are more draining?

There is nothing that exists in this universe that can cause us to experience shame except our own minds. Similarly, there is nothing in this universe that can make us feel appreciation except for our own minds.

Words like "shame" and "appreciation" are just concepts that we created and of which lack any inherent meaning; it is us that give these and other concepts meaning. When we remove these labels from the emotions that we experience, all that we have left is energy. It is the meaning that we give to our experience in relationships that create the fluctuations in the frequencies of our life's energy.

Your relationships are providing you with a mirror to how you interpret your experience. No relationship can make you feel anything; it is you that projects meaning on the other person. The quality of that meaning is determined by your vibratory level.

Because we attract that which is of the same vibratory level, everything that enters our lives, including our relationships, will be affected by that vibratory level.

By learning to control your vibratory level, you can raise your vibration to attract people into your life who are also of a higher vibration, and you can affect the vibratory level of those who you are in a relationship with already.

Chapter 8: When the Lines of Communication is Crossed

There are people who have sincerely used the Law of Attraction to find Mr. or Miss.

Right, but ended up with something less than satisfactory. As stated later, we are manifesting all the time; it is impossible for us to not manifest.

We may believe that the Law of Attraction does not work, that it is just a New Age talking point, or that we just lack some ability that others have. The only reason why we attract that which we do not want is because we are not directing your focus in a manner that supports us.

Not doing the work

If the person of your dreams is a 10 but your life condition is a 3, there is no way that you will be able to attract that person into your life and maintain a relationship with them.

If you want a partner that is a 10, you need to focus on becoming a 10 yourself. In fact, regardless of what you want in a partner, you need to be at least at their energetic level.

Remember, you attract into your life that which matches your frequency.

Attachment to outcome

Earlier in this book, I gave two personal examples that I had in trying out the Law of Attraction.

The first one was a success where I encountered a magazine cover that I had visualized.

The second attempt was unsuccessful because I had become attached to my outcome. The key to manifesting anything in your life is to create the intention for it, release that intention, and then move on with your life, don't spend time thinking about it.

Conscious beliefs

Imagine this scenario: You have been studying the Law of Attraction and you want to attract that special person.

You quiet your mind, create your intention, and go on with your life. As you are waiting for that special person to enter your life, you engage in thinking like:

- "I wonder if I am doing this (Law of Attraction) right?"
- *"What happens if doesn't work?"*
- "Maybe I am fooling myself about this manifesting thing."
- *"Things never work out for me. Why should this?"*
- "What happens if the person of my dreams shows up and I am not ready for them?"

If most of this person's focus is on thoughts such as these, then that will affect the level of their frequency that they are transmitting to the greater consciousness.

If you want to effectively use the Law of Attraction, you need to take charge of your beliefs and replace them with more empowering ones. We will discuss how to do this in Chapter 13.

Subconscious beliefs

One of the most important principles for learning how to use the Law of Attraction is the understanding of how subconscious beliefs impact our ability to attract that which we desire.

Even if you understand the importance of focusing on what you want, even if you create your intentions and become detached from them, you will not attract what you want if you have not explored your subconscious beliefs.

I want to start off this discussion by first saying that there is no such thing as a "subconscious" or "conscious" belief. Terms like "subconscious," "conscious" or "greater consciousness" are just concepts that we have created. As manifested beings, we use concepts to communicate our experiences to each other.

However, concepts are a creation of the mind, which is also a concept. There is no way that we can communicate without the use of concepts.

The problem is not the use of concepts, which are necessary to get along in this world. Problems arise when we identify with our concepts when we accept them as being true. Just as shadows were to the allegory of the cave, concepts are to our daily lives; they are experienced but they are not truth.

The following is a simple exercise that will allow you to briefly experience life free of concepts:

1. Sit down and view your surroundings, taking your time to take everything in.

2. When you are ready, close your eyes and allow yourself to relax.

3. Imagine that you are an alien from a distant planet who has arrived on Earth to study it. You have no information about this planet, nor do you have any past experience to draw from. Because of this, you are unable to define, identify, analyze, or judge anything that you experience. In other words, you are a blank slate.

4. No open your eyes and look at your surroundings again. Take your time.

5. How did your experience observing compare with your first observation?

If you did not notice any difference between the two observations, practice this exercise until you do.

The higher you raise your vibratory level, the less you will identify with your concepts. The less you identify with your concepts, the greater will be your experience of reality. As your experience of reality becomes greater, you will become aware of all of the universe.

Now that we have laid some ground work let us discuss how subconscious beliefs affect our ability to attract that which we desire. We will do so using the following scenario.

Janet was born to parents who were authoritarian and critical of her and her siblings. Like all children, Janet wanted their approval but nothing was ever good enough for her. By nature, Janet was very friendly and loved to explore new things. However, these natural qualities of her gradually diminished as Janet became more self-critical of herself. She had taken what was given to her by her parents and had directed it toward herself.

Janet cultivated this critical aspect of herself until it became her dominant personality. Because she is self-critical, she is also critical of others. The natural qualities of being friendly and loving to explore were suppressed in her subconscious; she lacks any awareness of them.

Based on the Law of Attraction, you would think that Janet would attract people in her life who were also self-critical; however, this is not necessarily the case.

Janet's qualities of being friendly and loving to explore, while being repressed, still give off their energetic vibration. Because she is unaware of these qualities, they will actually have a stronger impact in what manifests in her life!

This is why we sometimes see a couple who seem so different from each other that we find it puzzling how they ever got to together. This is also the reason why sometimes we have an instant dislike or attraction toward someone one who we do not even know.

All of these are examples of how our suppressed beliefs trump our conscious beliefs or intention as to what we want to attract in our lives. In Chapter 13, you have an opportunity to do an exercise to uncover your subconscious beliefs.

Remember to grab your free complimentary resources available at: www.LOAforSuccess.com

Chapter 9: The Face of God

You are the face of God. This statement that I just made may seem provocative and may offend some of you.

My hope is that, by the time that you complete this book, you will understand my reasons for making this statement, for it's at heart of not only understanding the Law of Attraction but your truest essence.

Also, when I use the word "God," I am not making reference to any specific religious belief, or preconceptions as to the nature of God, except one. That preconception is that there must be a source from which everything that exists arises from.

I want you to do the following exercise as I believe it can help you understand why I have repeatedly made the comment that you are consciousness.

It may also help facilitate your understanding to what I meant by "You are the face of God." But first, I need provide some important instructions: When conducting this exercise, do not rely on anything that you know, or that you think you know. Do not refer to memory or guessing.

Also, do not employ your imagination either. During this exercise, I want you only to refer to your immediate and direct experience.

1. Sit down, make yourself comfortable, and close your eyes.

2. Breathe normally, and follow your breath until you feel relaxed.

3. Now open your eyes and, with a relaxed gaze, look around at your surroundings.

4. Now find an object that interests you or attracts your attention.

5. As you look at the object, I want you to allow the object to come to your attention, rather than directing your attention at the object. In other words, look at the object with a relaxed gaze.

6. As you look at the objects, determine for yourself as to whether the act of seeing ends at the point where the object begins or does the act of seeing and the object merge into each other.

7. My hope is that you will agree that the act of seeing and the object seen merge into each other.

8. Now determine for yourself whether the act of seeing occurs from within you, or does it originate from outside of you. My hope is that you agree that the act of seeing originates from within you.

9. So far, I hope that you have come to the conclusion that seeing and the object being seen cannot be separated from each other; they are one. Also, that seeing occurs from within you.

10. You are aware of the object. Now determine for yourself if there is an awareness of seeing. My hope is that you will agree that there is an awareness of seeing.

11. Now determine for yourself if awareness of seeing and the act of seeing are separate from each other or if they are one. My hope you will agree that the awareness of seeing and the act of seeing are one.

12. How is that you were able to answer these questions? You were able to answer these questions by way of thought, thoughts like "seeing and the object seen merge into each other."

13. You are aware of thought. Determine for yourself whether the awareness of thought and thought itself are separate or are they one. My hope is that you will agree that these two things are one.

14. Now, are you aware of you? How do you know that you exist? You know that you exist, there is no disputing this. How do you know that you exist? You know that you exist because there is an awareness of you. Can you separate the awareness of you from you? My hope is that you agree that the awareness of you and that which you experience as being you, are one.

15. Now for the ultimate question, the question that surpasses all other questions: "Who or what is aware of you?" To be aware of something there must be the

object that is being perceived and the perceiver of the object.

16. If you are aware of you, then that which you refer to as "You" must be the object of awareness; but, you cannot be both the perceiver and the perceived.

17. My first guidance to you was to determine if seeing and the object being seen are separate or do they merge together. This is the question that you must ask yourself now. Is the awareness of that which you refer to as "you" and that which you refer to as "you" separate or do they merge together?

My hope is that you agree that they merge together. That which you refer to as "you" is the localized manifestation of the greater consciousness. That which is aware of "you" is the larger consciousness, the essence of who you are.

This essence of who you are cannot be perceived by the mind or the five senses.

It can only be known intuitively. It is this aspect of you that is aware of all existence.

It is aware of the objects around you. It is aware of the act of seeing. It is aware of the awareness of seeing. It is aware of that which is within you and around you, and it is aware of that which you refer to as "you," which is just another object floating in the unlimited field of consciousness. Consciousness is aware of all of existence while at the same time being intimately connected to all of existence.

Nothing can exist unless there is an awareness of it. This is why I made the statement that you are the "face of god." Everything that you experience, be it a rock, a fly, or another person, is the face of god, a god that expresses itself in innumerable forms.

Chapter 10: The Mirror of Relationships

As the face of god, which is your manifested form, it is the purpose of your life to wake-up from the dream that is created by the mind that leads us to believe that we are just a physical body with a mind.

It is your purpose to wake-up from the dream that you are separate from the rest of life and return to wholeness and oneness of being, which is the greater consciousness.

The return to wholeness and oneness does not require us to dismiss the physicality of our bodies or the physical realm that we find ourselves in. It does not require that we die and merge with some spiritual realm.

It does not mean we have to abandon our current lifestyle and become monks or adopt spiritual practices. The return to wholeness and oneness is an inner journey where we gain the courage to challenge the deep seated beliefs that we have of ourselves and learn to let go of them.

The greater consciousness, or god, is the ultimate manifester because it lacks any sense of identity or beliefs about itself; it is simply pure awareness.

At this level, just an intention manifests into existence instantly. As manifested beings of the greater consciousness, we too can manifest; however, our manifestations do not occur instantly as there is lag time involved.

This lag time is due to the restrictions imposed by the physical realm and because of the ego. Our beliefs that we have about ourselves and others creates resistance, which creates lag time for our manifestations to appear.

The more that we overcome our inner resistance, the more effective we will become in manifesting. Fortunately, the universe has offered us the ultimate mirror for recognizing resistance, that mirror is our relationships.

As indicated earlier, the people who enter our lives did so because there was a vibrational match to ours.

Since the vibrational match may come from subconscious beliefs, identifying that vibrational frequency is not impossible unless we explore our subconscious beliefs. Regardless if the beliefs are conscious or subconscious, we project those beliefs on others, which then becomes our image of them. In truth, we can never know another person. From the perspective of our "normal" level of consciousness, we never have a relationship with another person; rather, we have a relationship with our interpretation of them.

It is because of our projections that we make on others that the people in our lives serve as a mirror to our inner realm. When we realize this, we can understand why relationships are complicated and why misunderstandings occur.

We project our inner lives on the people around us, which then becomes our image of them. When they do not meet our expectations, we become hurt or frustrated; we hold them responsible for our unhappiness.

Because the collective consciousness of the world has only recently (evolutionary speaking) begin to rise toward higher levels, ours is a history that viewed relationships not as mirrors but as objects for experiencing fulfillment and wholeness.

From fairy tales to Hollywood, from romance novels to the traditions that we uphold, we have looked to find Mr. or Miss Right to deliver us from our sense of separation from the world and to make us feel loved, desired and whole. Such a recipe for finding happiness is doomed to failure. No person or object outside of you can ever give you want you are looking for.

To do so is no different than asking your mirror at home to provide you with love and fulfillment. Everything that you will ever experience is a projection of yourself that becomes superimposed on the object of our experience.

Ultimately, everything that you experience is an aspect of yourself. Ultimately, you are the source of all experience as well as being found in all of experience. It is like a person who sprays their garden with a hose.

Everything in the garden is covered with water and water become an aspect of every plant. Consciousness is to water as the garden is to experience. Everything that you could ever desire already exists within the realm of consciousness because consciousness is the source of all that exists.

 The Law of Attraction is just a conceptual model for how consciousness operates. The only thing that prevents us from being intentional creators is the limiting concepts that we identify with due to our attachment to our manifested form.

Ultimately freedom lies in transcending all beliefs, including spiritual beliefs, and opening up to all of experience with complete acceptance and abandon.

Finding your true love or the relationship of your dream requires that you stop searching for it and investigate the timeless and boundless realm that exists within you and is you. To experience that realm, the most effective tool is meditation.

Chapter 11: Using the Law of Attraction in Relationships

We have covered a lot of information so far. It is time make this information practical and apply it to your current and potential relationships. There are three simple steps to applying the Law of Attraction:

1. Identify what you want your outcome to be.
2. Identify what has prevented you from achieving your relationship outcome in the past.
3. Raise your vibration

You can think of your relationship outcome as your intention. When you identify the limiting beliefs that have prevented you from achieving your relationship outcome in the past, you can then raise your vibration.

When we change our limiting beliefs and adopt empowering ones, we raise our vibration. By raising your vibration, you increase the probability that you will manifest your intentions.

Here is an example of how this process works. My relationship outcome is to improve the quality of my relationship with my spouse.

I would ask myself "What has prevented me from improving my relationship with my wife/husband in the past? In the next chapter, I have provided you with a number of exercises that you can use to identify your underlying beliefs.

Upon identifying your belief, I would next raise my vibration. All of the exercises in Chapter 13 can be used to raise your vibration. In fact, all of the exercises in this chapter can be used to raise your vibration. It is important to note that these steps do not always have followed in this order. Sometimes raising your vibration can lead you to identify your beliefs.

By raising your vibration, and maintaining it, along with releasing your intention, you will be intentionally manifesting your relationship outcome. Here are some examples of how you can apply *the Law of Attraction in Relationships*:

- Attracting a compatible partner: Think of the qualities that you want in a partner; you can be specific as possible. Consider all the attributes you would desire in a partner, including physically, emotionally, mentally, spiritually, and financially. When you have identified these qualities, make them the focus of your intention.

- Improving the quality of an existing relationship: To improve an existing relationship, you must first start off by asking yourself some questions about you! Ask questions like:
    - Would I want to be in a relationship with someone who was just like me?
    - *How have I contributed to the challenges that we are currently experiencing in our relationship?*
    - What beliefs do I hold about myself and the other person that are creating challenges for the relationship?
    - *How have I contributed to the unhappiness of my partner?*
    - How have my own beliefs contributed to my own unhappiness?

After acknowledging your role in creating relationship challenges, you can create the intentions that will bring happiness for both you and your partner.

It is important in relationship challenges that your intentions be pure and unconditional, meaning that your intentions for your partner's happiness are independent of your own needs. In fact, when releasing your intentions, do not even consider the relationship; consider the happiness of the individual.

To make your intentions even more powerful, let your intentions be how you can contribute to the happiness of the other person. Likewise, you can create intentions for your own happiness, using the same methods just described but with you as the focus.

It is important; however that I make the following qualifier. If you are in an abusive relationship, emotionally or physically, do not employ the Law of Attraction in an attempt to save the relationship.

As I stated before, everything starts with us. We attract into our life that which is a match for our vibration. Before you can change anything, you must change yourself first, and to change yourself means to change your vibration.

You cannot do this if you are in an unsafe situation. Take care of yourself first, and the universe will accommodate the changes that you make.

Chapter 12: Conscious Relationships

Many spiritual teachings that are available; however, which teaching is best? Why do some spiritual teachings contradict each other? Why do some spiritual teachings resonate with us, while others leave us uninterested?

The answers to all of these questions can be known by considering the following: Spiritual teachings are just another form of thought, and we attract those teachings into our lives that best fit us at the given moment of our conscious awareness.

The best spiritual teaching is the one that resonates with you. Spiritual teachings contradict each other because everyone is at a different place in their evolution of consciousness.

What one person is ready to hear will be unsuitable for another person. Everything that we attract into our lives, be they relationships or spiritual teachings, has entered because it was a vibrational match to our frequency.

What most people who practice the Law of Attraction fail to realize is that they are focusing on the small and limited scale instead of focusing on the ultimate prize, which is becoming firmly established in your true essence.

You can attract money; you can attract relationships or anything else you could want. But as long as we are focusing on attracting what we want, we are missing the opportunity to attract the realization of who we truly are!

When we realize this, we will not even think of the Law of Attraction or relationships. Instead, we will be focusing on how we can serve and elevate others for a more compassionate, more loving, and more highly evolved society where we support each other in our own growth, which is how a conscious relationship functions.

Conscious relationships are drastically different from the traditional relationships that most of us are involved in. In traditional relationships, we look to our partner to fulfill our needs and expectations.

In conscious relationships, we do not look to our partner to fulfill our needs and expectations; we realize that no one can fulfill our needs or expectations except ourselves. In traditional relations, we may feel threatened if our partner wants to pursue their desires when we do not share those same desires. In conscious relationships, we encourage our partner to pursue their desires, even if it could potentially cause them to leave us.

The foundational characteristic of a conscious relationship is that the partners support each other in discovering their own truth.

Conscious relationships are the ultimate mirror because there is a common understanding that relationships are not about depending on the other person to make us feel fulfilled; rather, it is about providing our support to the other person so that they can discover the fulfillment that lies within themselves.

The Power of Meditation

Unfortunately, the practice of meditation has been widely misunderstood, both culturally and spiritually. Meditation originated with the indigenous people of India, before the creation of its major religions like Hinduism and Buddhism.

In its original form, meditation was used as a vehicle to connect with the original source of all that is. Meditation was not used to reduce stress and relax but to transcend the mind and experience our inherent connection to all of existence.

In the Western world, the practice of meditation and yoga have been popularized as way to achieve a certain outcome such as improved mental, emotional, or physical well being.

However, this approach has just reinforced the misunderstanding what we are just physical beings that inhabit a physical world.

Compare this perspective to the perspective that we are multidimensional beings, that we are consciousness that has manifested as localized consciousness and having physical form.

It is our conceptual thinking and the beliefs that we have of ourselves that prevent most of us from experiencing both aspects of ourselves.

From perspective of pure consciousness, you do not do meditation; rather, you are the one that is observing the meditator. As pure consciousness, you become whatever your intentions are. As previously stated, you are an aspect in all that you experience.

In combination with relationships, meditation becomes another mirror in your arsenal of self-realization tools. Meditation, in its purest form, is discovering who you are at deepest level and your relationship to all of existence, which is more substantial and fulfilling than a method for reducing stress!

When practicing the kind of meditation that I have been describing, the idea is to transcend all concepts and thinking. The exercises in Chapter 13, if followed in the sequence that they are ordered, offer you the opportunity to transcend how you experience yourself and the world around you.

If what I have written so far seems too abstract or deep, don't let that bother you. Words are just concepts.

As stated earlier, the best guide to experiencing realignment with your higher power is to learn to develop greater awareness to your feelings and to learn to trust them.

When we learn to become in tune with our feelings and trust them, we have taken a major step toward attaining enlightenment, also known as loving yourself. The next chapter offers meditative exercises for raising your vibration and lowering your resistance.

Chapter 13: Law of Attraction Exercises for Relationships

We have covered a lot of information in this book, and it is time to put that information into practice. The following are exercises that will benefit you by identifying your limiting beliefs, changing your limiting beliefs, lowering your resistance, developing greater awareness of the nature of your mental phenomena, becoming aware of your projections, and enhancing your ability to experience love and compassion for yourself and others.

There is no specific way to approach these exercises. You can pick the ones that resonate with you, or you can do all of them.

For best results, I recommend that you do all of the exercises and that you do them in the order that they are sequenced. I have staggered these exercises from simplest to the most difficult, especially for meditation exercises.

Exercises for Beliefs

Uncovering deep seated beliefs

Previously in this book, we discussed subconscious beliefs and how they impact the manifestation process. The following are two exercises for uncovering your subconscious beliefs:

Exercise 1

To show you how this exercise works, I will provide you with an example.

1. The first step is to think of an ongoing challenge that you are experiencing in your life. My example will be: *I am afraid of being rejected by others.*
2. My next step is to start a line of inquiry using the phrase "What would be so bad if..." So my first question would be "What would be so bad about being rejected?"
3. My answer to that question would be "I would feel that people saw me as being less, that I am not good enough.
4. I would then use my response and rephrase the question: "What would be so bad if people saw me as being less or not good enough?"
5. My response to that would be "It would make feel like I am worthless."
6. I would continue to repeat this question by asking: "What would be so bad if I felt like I am worthless?"

7. My answer to that would be "I would feel like I am unlovable."

8. Keep going through this line of questioning until you are unable to any further. When you have reached this point, you will have identified your subconscious belief. At the conscious level, I am aware of the fear of being rejected; however, the core belief behind this belief is "I feel like I am unlovable."

Exercise 2:

This next exercise can be used to find the subconscious beliefs for the things that we want. For this exercise, I will use the example: "I want to get married."

1. What would getting married give me?
2. It would give me someone to spend my life with.
3. What would having someone to spend my life with give me?
4. It would give me a sense of security.
5. What would a sense of security give me?
6. It would give me a sense of peace.
7. My subconscious belief is that I want a sense of peace, but my conscious belief is that I want to get married.

Habitual Patterns

1. Start becoming more aware of your daily thinking and actions.

2. When you catch yourself thinking a habitual thought or behaving habitually, ask yourself the following questions:

    a. Do I have a choice of thinking or behaving differently?

    b. Is there a payoff for me thinking or behaving in this habitual way?

    c. How would I like to think as opposed to my current habitual thinking?

    d. How would I like to behave as opposed to my current habitual behavior?

    e. Would these new ways of thinking or behaving retain the payoff that my current thinking or behaving offers?

    f. Would these new ways of thinking or behaving bring me greater happiness?

3. If you said yes to the last two questions, start incorporating your new way of thinking or behaving in your daily life.

4. Whenever you catch yourself repeating your old thinking or behaving, remind yourself that you are now dedicated to your new ways of being.

Changing a Belief

When you have identified a belief that is limiting you (subconscious or conscious), you can use the following procedure to weaken your old belief and replace it with a more empowering belief:

1. Get two sheets of paper. Select paper sizes of 8" x 11" or larger.

2. Take the first sheet of paper and fold it in half lengthwise.

3. On the top of the paper, write down your belief.

4. Make a list on the left-hand side of the paper of all the ways this belief has cost you in your life. When doing this part of the exercise, think of how this belief has affected you in all your life areas. Ask yourself how this belief has affected you in the way that you see yourself, how it has affected your emotional health, your relationships, your physical health, your work, your finances, and so on.

5. When writing, keep in mind the following:

- When writing this list, write down the first thing that comes to your mind, even if it seems irrelevant.

- Write as fast as you can and feel the emotions that arise. This is a heartfelt exercise, not a thinking one.

- Keep writing until you run out of things to write.

6. By each item that you write down, assign an arbitrary point value as to how much impact this item has had on you. When selecting the point value, choose the first number that comes to mind.

7. When you have completed assigning the point values, find the total of all the point values and place it at the bottom of the page.

8. For the right side of the page, repeat Steps 6-7, except this time, you will write down all the ways that this belief has benefited you.

When you have completed Step 8, think of a new alternative belief that empowers you. For example, if the original belief was "No one will ever love me," my new belief maybe "The only love that I can depend on is the love that I give to myself."

On the second paper, repeat steps 1-8, using your new belief, with the following exceptions: Reverse Steps 6 and 8 by writing down all the ways that you believe that you would benefit from this new belief for Step 6. When doing Step 8, write down all the ways you believe it will cost you.

When you have completed the two sheets, do the following:

1. Immediately review your lists, allowing yourself to fully experience any emotions that arise.

2. Review yours lists every day, once in the morning and once before you go to bed until you become fully associated with the emotions that you experience.

When you become fully associated with the costs for holding on to your old belief with the benefits of adopting your new belief, your mind will become re-programmed with your new belief.

The following is an alternative to the last exercise for changing your beliefs and involves meditation:

1. On the piece of paper, write down a belief that you have which limits you or is causing you unhappiness.

2. When you have written down the belief, sit down in a comfortable position and close your eyes.

3. Allow yourself to follow your breath during inhalation and exhalation. Place your attention on your breath. Feel it as it courses through your body. Relax.

4. I want you to think of the belief that you wrote down. Feel the heaviness and the weight, which this belief has had on your life.

5. What has been the cost to your happiness for holding on to this belief? Can you think of specific instances? Did this belief cost you a relationship? If so, who is no longer in your life because of this belief?

6. Has this belief cost you money? Did this belief lead you to engage in risky behavior with your money or health? What about your sense of self?

7. How has this belief affected your self-confidence or self-esteem? Take the time to feel the pain that this belief has created for your life.

8. Allow yourself to experience it fully, allow yourself to experience the emotions and feelings that come with living with this belief.

9. How will this belief affect your future? If you continue to hold on to this belief, what will your life be like a year from now, five years from now, 15 years from now? See your life in the future. What consequences will you experience if you continue to maintain this belief?

10. As mentioned before, thoughts and beliefs do not have any power other than the power we give them. Unto

themselves, our thoughts and beliefs lack any power. Our beliefs are not true or untrue, they just exist. It is us who grant them power over our lives.

11. Now open your eyes and get your writing instrument. This negative belief you just meditated on existed because you perceived in your mind that there was a benefit to having this belief.

12. Write down how all the ways this belief benefited you, even if how it benefited does not sound rationale. For example, if you have a belief that you cannot depend on or trust other people, the benefit of this belief may be that it protected you from getting hurt.

13. Now think of a belief that will offer the same benefit but will not create limitations for you. Using the previous example, a new belief could be "I can trust others because I am learning to trust myself." Write down your new belief.

14. When you have written down the belief, sit down in a comfortable position and close your eyes.

15. Allow yourself to follow your breath during inhalation and exhalation. Place your attention on your breath. Feel it as it courses through your body. Relax.

16. I want you to think of the new belief that you wrote down. Think about what your life would be like if you operated from this new belief from this moment on.

17. How would living with this new belief make you feel about yourself? How would it impact those that you care about? What would your life be like? Think about what your life would be like one year from now if you started to live by this new belief today. What do you think it would be like five years from now?

18. As you think about what your life would be like, allow yourself to experience the emotions and feelings that you experience. Allow yourself to sink into these emotions and feelings. You may want to visualize yourself acting from this new belief.

19. Practice this meditation every day for three weeks, which is how long it normally takes to create a habit. The mind cannot tell the difference between visualization and actual doing. Meditating regularly will reprogram your subconscious, leading you to take the appropriate action.

20. Start becoming more aware of your daily thinking and actions.

21. When you catch yourself thinking a habitual thought or behaving habitually, ask yourself the following questions:

    a. Do I have a choice of thinking or behaving differently?

    b. Is there a payoff for me thinking or behaving in this habitual way?

    c. How would I like to think as opposed to my current habitual thinking?

    d. How would I like to behave as opposed to my current habitual behavior?

    e. Would these new ways of thinking or behaving retain the payoff that my current thinking or behaving offers?

    f. Would these new ways of thinking or behaving bring me greater happiness?

22. If you said yes to the last two questions, start incorporating your new way of thinking or behaving in your daily life.

23. Whenever you catch yourself repeating your old thinking or behaving, remind yourself that you are now dedicated to your new ways of being.

Exercises for Emotions

Diving Deep into Emotions

We discussed earlier that emotions are a mirror to our thoughts. We also discussed how our subconscious beliefs can override our intentions to manifest. The purpose of this exercise is to guide you in transforming your emotions at their deepest level; thus, changing them at the subconscious level.

1. Identify a concern that you are experiencing. Since this book is about relationships, I will use the following concern as an example: I am frustrated with my child being irresponsible.

2. Now that I have identified my concern, the next thing would be to identify how I feel about the situation, which I have done already.

3. Upon identifying how I feel about the situation, the next thing to do is to get into a relaxed state. Using the basic meditation that was presented earlier in this book is ideal for this.

4. When you are relaxed, ask yourself "What does being frustrated feel like?" Notice: You want to describe what the emotion feels like, not what you think about it. To avoid

falling into this trap, phrase your response as "It feels like_____?

5. Here are some examples:

6. "It feels hard and edgy."

7. "I feel like I want to cry."

8. "It feels heavy."

9. My response to this question would be that feeling frustrated feels heavy, like I am being pulled down."

10. I would then follow-up by asking "What does heavy or being pulled down feel like?"

11. I would then respond with "It feels like I am stuck."

12. I would continue my questioning by asking "What does being stuck feel like?"

13. My response: "Feeling stuck makes me feel like I want to go to sleep or escape."

14. I would follow-up by asking "What does going to sleep or escaping feel like?"

15. My response would be "It feels like I am freeing myself."

16. My last response, "It feels like I am freeing myself" has a whole different feeling than my initial feeling, which was

feeling frustrated. When your line of questioning leads you to feeling a neutral or positive emotion, you have transformed your original emotion at its deepest level.

17. When doing this exercise, it is important to mention that there is no way that you can do it wrong or come up with the wrong answer. As long as you are responding at the feeling level, your response will be valid for this exercise.

Exercises for Resistance

Allowing of the body

The following exercise is good for learning to be mindful of your body. To do this exercise, do the following:

1. Sit in a chair or on a pillow and allow yourself to be comfortable.
2. Close your eyes and relax.
3. Allow your awareness to roam freely; do not try to focus on anything particular.
4. Now place your awareness on the body. Allow your body to move any way it wants. Do not try in any way to control your posture or the way you are sitting. Whatever your body is telling you, allow your body to assume that movement or positioning.
5. Enjoy the allowing of your body. Maintain this allowing for as long as you desire.

A Day without Resistance

It is the resistance that we create within ourselves that prevent us from experiencing our full potential for manifesting. All of us, at one point or another, have engaged in actions that went against how we felt.

The purpose of this exercise is to start honoring your feelings by only engaging in those actions that are consistent with how you feel.

To live your life in accordance to how you feel is to be in alignment, which eliminates resistance. It is important to note that this exercise is about feelings, not emotions. If we lived according to our emotions, the results could be troublesome.

Unlike your emotions, your feelings are those messages that are guiding you to either move toward a situation or to move away from it. You can think of feelings as "approaching for avoiding.

I want you to commit to one day where you will only engage in those activities that are consistent with how you feel. If you do not feel like doing something, then do not do it. If you are feeling like doing something, do it! If you find yourself having trouble doing this exercise for a whole day, then do it for a shorter period of time, even if it is for just 20 minutes then extend that time until you can do it for a whole day.

Obviously, there are things that we need to do which we rather not do. To not do them would not be irresponsible. In cases such as these, use the following guidelines:

-Change your perspective of the task that is creating resistance in you by focusing on all the benefits that you would gain by completing it.

-Find ways to change the way that you approach doing the task by making it more enjoyable for you. Example: Listen to your favorite music while doing yard work or invite a friend over to do your taxes together.

-If none of the previous techniques work, do not take on the task until you have come to accept the fact that you need to do this task and that it will not be enjoyable. Regarding this technique, I want you to focus on the word "accept." It means you do the task with complete acceptance for what it is; you have lost any sense putting up a fight against it.

-These guidelines lead to an important point. This exercise has nothing to do with the activities that we do; rather, it is about recognizing the resistance that we experience and honoring it.

Exercises for Relationships

Projections

From the perspective of higher levels of consciousness, there is no distinction between your inner world and the world around you.

All relationship problems occur when we experience others as being separate from ourselves and mistakenly believe that which we project on them originates from them. The following is a meditation for reclaiming your projections.

Exercise 1: Projections

1. Sit down in a comfortable position, close your eyes, and relax.

2. Follow your breath during inhalation and exhalation.

3. When you are feeling calm, I want you to think of someone whom you believe has treated you unfairly. When you have identified this person, I want you to recreate in your mind the specific situation where this person mistreated you.

4. Where did the situation take place?

5. Imagine the surroundings of this location.

6. Where was this person when the situation happened? What were they doing at the time? See it in your mind; visualize it with as much detail as possible.

7. What did they say or do to you that caused you to be angry or hurt?

8. How did you feel when the situation happened? What did it feel like? What did you tell yourself?

9. Now I want you to recreate this same situation in your mind with one difference. I want you to relieve the situation without any form of judgment or analysis.

10. As you run through the situation a second time in your mind, focus on the other person that you believe hurt you. Can you say that you are absolutely sure that this person intended to hurt you? Is it possible that you were projecting your own beliefs on this person's intent?

11. If while reliving the situation you experiencing hurt or anger, from where do these feelings arise? Did this person impose these feelings on you, or are these feelings generated from within you?

12. The hurt that you believe that this person caused you, whether they intended to so or not, are you not

committing the same offense against yourself at this moment? How long will you continue to carry this hurt?

Exercise 2: Projections

1. Think of a people in your life who have qualities about them that bother you.

2. When you have identified the qualities, write them down on a piece of paper. I recommend that you use one piece of paper for each quality that you identify.

3. For each quality, write out all the reasons why this quality bothers you. For example, if the quality is that the other person is insensitive, you could write something like this:

4. By being insensitive, you make the world colder. It can lead to others feeling hurt, and it prevents you from experiencing the emotions and feelings of others. Being insensitive is like living in a barren desert.

5. Remember that how you experience the outer world around is a reflection of your inner world. That which bothers you in others is also found to some degree within you as well. If you are disturbed the insensitivity of others, it is because you have insensitivity within

you, and you associated emotional pain to being insensitive.

6. Now reflect on the benefits of having that quality that you find bothersome in the other person, if not to a smaller degree.

7. Using the previous example, a benefit of having a degree of insensitivity in you may be that you would not be bothered by what other people think of you. You might not be less reactive emotionally, or you may feel a greater degree freedom in doing what you want to do without worrying about what other people might say.

8. By acknowledging the nobility of your subconscious aspects, that which you are keeping suppressed, you relinquish your resistance to it. In doing this, it will lose its potency as a counterforce when you are using your conscious mind to attract what which you desire.

Compassion

What of the most fundamental qualities that are needed for a healthy relationship is compassion? You may think of love as the most important quality for a relationship; however, love is often experienced as being conditional. In other words, we have a thought that goes like this: "I will love you as long as you_____." You can fill-in the blank. Compassion is unconditional; you feel compassion for another because you can connect to their suffering. The following is an exercise for expanding your compassion. This exercise is a series of sub exercises, with each one creating the foundation for the following exercise.

Step 1:

I want you to think of a person or animal that you love. When you have identified the subject of this reflection, I want you to think of all the ways that you appreciate them. Experience the feelings and emotions that you have for your subject and fully experience them. I want you to think of all the hardships and challenges that they have experienced. Think of the sufferings that they have experienced and make their suffering your own. When you have connected with their sufferings, express your love to them and wish them happiness.

Step 2:

In this next exercise, you are going to repeat what you did in the first exercise; however, this time you are going to choose a subject that you have neutral feelings for. For example, your subject could be the clerk at the register where you do your shopping or the mailperson. Even though you may not know anything about this person, I want you to imagine the sufferings that they may have experienced in their life. Use your intuition or your imagination but make their suffering as real for you can. Allow yourself to experience their sufferings as your own. When you have connected with their sufferings, express your love to them and wish them happiness.

Step 3:

In this third exercise, you are going to repeat what you did in the last two exercises; however, using another subject. In this exercise, your subject is going to be someone who you dislike, avoid, or you do not get along with. I want you to think of the sufferings that they have experienced in their life. As in the previous exercise, you can use your intuition or imagination if you do not know this person's background. Allow yourself to experience their sufferings as your own. When you have connected with their sufferings, express your love to them and wish them happiness.

Step 4:

This exercise differs from the previous three exercises because you will not be identifying your subject ahead of time. Instead, you perform this compassion exercise as you go about your day. I want you to notice the people around you as you conduct your daily business. Take time to imagine the potential sufferings of the people that you see. Allow yourself to experience their sufferings as your own. When you have connected with their sufferings, express your love to them and wish them happiness.

Step 5:

This is the final exercise, and for many people, the most difficult one. In this exercise, you will be the subject of your reflection. I want you to reflect on the sufferings that you have experienced in your life. Allow yourself to experience your sufferings fully; do not minimize anything. Get in touch with pains that you have experienced. When you have connected with your own sufferings, express love to yourself and wish yourself happiness.

The exercise that you just completed was an exercise in experiencing compassion, and the subject of your compassion began with the ones that are the easiest for us to experience compassion for, those whom we love. Each succeeding exercise became more difficult because the subject of your compassion became further removed from you emotionally. Most people have trouble loving or showing compassion for themselves, which is why you were the subject of the final meditation.

The power of your compassion for others is dependent on your ability to have compassion for yourself. When we lack compassion for others it is because we lack compassion for ourselves; we project our lack of compassion for ourselves on those who are around us.

Conversely, when you develop compassion for yourself, you can truly have compassion for others. The power of compassion is also vital if you are to become an intentional manifester because compassion increases your vibration to a high level.

***

Meditation Exercises

One of the most effective ways to raise your vibrational level is through meditation. Mediation allows us to expand your awareness of your mental phenomena such as thoughts, perceptions, and sensations. By developing greater awareness of your mental phenomena, you will weaken your sense of identification with them. By losing your identification of them, you will lower your resistance toward them. By lowering your resistance, you raise your vibrational level. We will start off with a basic meditation.

Basic Meditation

1. Sit down either on the floor or in a chair and make yourself comfortable.

2. Allow yourself to relax and close your eyes as you breathe normally.

3. Place your awareness on the sensations that you experience as your breath flows into your body during inhalation and flows out of your body during exhalation.

4. As you focus on your breath, do not judge or analyze anything that you experience. Fully accept everything that you experience just as it is.

5. Whenever you get distracted by a thought, gently return your attention back to your breath, regardless of how many times you lose your concentration. With continued practice, your mind will become calmer as the amount of attention that you give your thoughts will become less and less.

Meditation on Thought

The purpose of this exercise is to expand your awareness to the nature of thought.

1. Make yourself comfortable, close your eyes, and relax.

2. Place your attention on your breath as you breathe normally.

3. As thoughts enter your awareness, observe them by maintaining your awareness of them. When observing your thoughts, do so without any sense of judgment or resistance. What happens to your thought when you observe them in this manner?

4. As you maintain the awareness of your thoughts, notice their qualities. Do your thoughts undergo changes or are they fixed and unchanging?

5. Where to do your thoughts appear from? Can you locate this place?

6. Where do your thoughts go when as they fade away from your awareness? Can you locate this place?

7. What do you experience when one thought fades away and your next thought has yet to appear?

8. This is the end of this exercise; continue meditating as long as you want.

Exercise 1: Emotions

The purpose of this meditation is to expand your awareness of your emotions.

1. Make yourself comfortable, close your eyes, and relax.

2. Place your attention on your breath as you breathe normally.

3. As you experience emotions, observe them by maintaining your awareness of them. When observing your emotions, do so without any sense of judgment or resistance. What happens to your emotions when you observe them in this manner? What do you notice?

4. As you maintain the awareness of your emotions, notice their qualities. Do your emotions undergo changes or are they fixed and unchanging?

5. Where to do your emotions appear from? Can you locate this place?

6. Where do your emotions go when as they fade away from your awareness? Can you locate this place?

7. What do you experience when one emotion fades away and your next emotion has yet to appear?

8. This is the end of this exercise; continue meditating as long as you want.

Exercise 2: Emotions

1. Sit down and make yourself comfortable.

2. Close your eyes and allow yourself to relax.

3. Place your attention on your breath as it enters and exits your body, focusing on the sensations you experience as you inhale and exhale.

4. Identify any negative emotions that you may be experiencing. If you are not experiencing a negative emotion, think of a problem or negative experience. When you experience a negative emotion, offer it total acceptance. Do not try to avoid it, deny it, or change it; allow the emotion to fully express itself.

5. Place your full awareness on the emotion, allow yourself to observe it with your attention but do not engage it. Allow yourself to experience the sensations that accompany the emotion. Pretend that you are diving into the emotion; allow yourself to become fully immersed in it. Remember, your emotions have no power as long as you do not try to resist them to or try to interpret them. As long as you involvement with them is restricted to observing them and experiencing them, you will be in charge.

6. What happens to the potency of your emotions when you just observe them and allow them to fully express themselves?

Feelings

Exercise 1: Feelings

The purpose of this exercise is to expand your awareness of your feelings.

1. Make yourself comfortable, close your eyes, and relax.

2. Place your attention on your breath as you breathe normally.

3. As you experience feelings in your body, observe them by maintaining your awareness of them. When observing your feelings, do so without any sense of judgment or resistance. What happens to your feelings when you observe them in this manner? What do you notice?

4. As you maintain the awareness of your feelings, notice their qualities. Do your feelings undergo changes or are they fixed and unchanging?

5. Where to do your feelings appear from? Can you locate this place?

6. Where do your feelings go when as they fade away from your awareness? Can you locate this place?

7. What do you experience when one feeling fades away and your next feeling has yet to appear?

8. This is the end of this exercise; continue meditating as long as you want.

Exercise 2: Feelings

We previously discussed how our feelings are like a GPS in that they indicate how aligned we are with the larger consciousness. The following meditation can be used to expand your awareness of your feelings.

1. Sit down, make yourself comfortable, and relax.

2. Breathe normally as you focus on your breath, just as you did in the basic meditation exercise.

3. As you become more relaxed, be aware of any feelings that you are experiencing.

4. Allow yourself to experience your feelings without any judgment. Do not try control or change any feeling that you experience. Do not classify any of your feelings as being good or bad, pleasant or unpleasant for these are value judgments that exist solely in the mind. I want you to just place your attention on the feelings that you experience.

5. Are the feelings that you experience stable? Are they always the same or do they change? Are they always there or do they come and go?

6. Just stay in the awareness of your feelings, allow yourself to experience them for as long as you desire.

7. This is the end of this meditation. Feel free to allow yourself to continue to meditate on the body for as long as you wish.

Beyond the Image of You

This final meditation is the ultimate meditation as it involves self-inquiry into the nature of your own existence. To understand the nature of your own existence is to challenge every belief that you have ever had about yourself and the world around you. As in all meditations, do not judge, criticize, or analyze any aspect of your experience. Greet every experience will complete acceptance. Do not turn to your knowledge, experience, imagination, or ideas during this meditation. Approach this exercise purely through your direct experience.

1. Make yourself comfortable and relax.

2. Close your eyes and place your attention on your breath.

3. Observe the perceptions, thoughts, sensations, feelings, and emotions that arise from within you. Notice how they come and go on their own, that they appear and fade away on their own accord.

4. Notice how these mental phenomena appear and fade away, but you, the observer of them, always remains.

5. Notice that perception, the ability to hear sound, and the ability to feel occur without any effort by you. These sensory functions occur without any of your involvement; you are the witness to these things.

6. The functions of your mind and body all carry on without any effort on your part. Who or what is aware of all of this?

7. If you tell yourself "I am the one who is aware of this," there must be an awareness of this answer. Who or what is aware of the response that you give? How can you be "I" when there is an awareness of this "I"? Where is this "I" located?

8. Who you are is the one that is aware of thought, sensations, perception, sound, and smell. Who you are is aware of every response that you give when conducting this inquiry. Who is this one? Regardless of how you respond to this question, there is awareness of it as well.

9. The word "phenomenal" means something that can be seen, thought, touched, heard, or detected somehow. The truth of who you are cannot be phenomenal. How can you be both the perceived and the perceiver? Who you are is non-phenomenal, for you are consciousness itself!

This book is also available in audio format.

You can learn more at:

www.LOAforSuccess.com/audiobooks

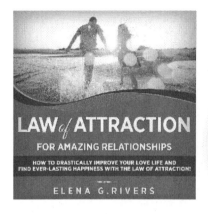

Conclusion

We are approaching the end of this book now. Remember that the Law of Attraction is not an end unto itself. It is just a normal function of the universe and we can learn to use it consciously. However, the greatest things happen after diving deep and developing more awareness.

Upon achieving higher levels of awareness, it will become crystal clear to you that who we are is beyond our thoughts. As pure consciousness, we can manifest anything we want spontaneously without bigger effort. In order to get there, get committed to getting to know your true self and removing resistance. Schedule your LOA rituals time and enjoy the exercises from this book. We are all energy. Let's rise higher and enjoy the process! I am very curious to hear back to you.

If you have a few moments, please share your thoughts in the review section of this book and let us know which exercise you found most helpful. Your honest review would be much appreciated. It's you I am writing for and I would love to know your feedback.

Enjoy your LOA journey,

Elena

A Special Offer from Elena

Finally, I would like to invite you to join my private mailing list (my **VIP LOA Newsletter**). Whenever I release a new book, you will be able to get it at a discounted price (or sometimes even for free, but don't tell anyone ☺).

In the meantime, I will keep you entertained with a free copy of my exclusive LOA workbook that will be emailed to you when you sign up.

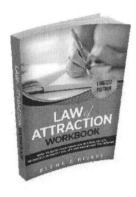

To join visit the link below now:

www.loaforsuccess.com/newsletter

After you have signed up, you will get a free instant access to this exclusive workbook (+ many other helpful resources that I will be sending you on a regular basis). I hope you will enjoy your free workbook.

If you have any questions, please email us at:
support@loaforsuccess.com

More Books written by Elena G.Rivers
Available at: www.LOAforSuccess.com

Law of Attraction for Weight Loss

Law of Attraction for Abundance

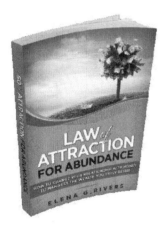

Law of Attraction to Make More Money

Law of Attraction -Manifestation Exercises

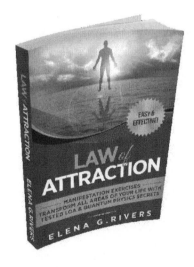

You will find more at:

www.loaforsuccess.com/books

All of our books are available in eBook, paperback, hardcover and audiobook formats.

To learn more, visit our website:

www.LOAforSuccess.com

Printed in Great
Britain
by Amazon